American Indians in the 1800s

Roben Alarcon, M.A.Ed.

Table of Contents

Growing Conflict

In the 1800s, America was a growing country. White settlers wanted more land. They felt the American Indians were getting in the way of progress. The Indian tribes had always roamed the land freely. They did not own land; they shared the land.

The two groups of people saw life very differently. Getting along became a struggle for people in the West. The government looked for ways to fix the problem. It decided to move the tribes to **reservations** (rez-uhr-VAY-shuhns). The Indians were not happy with this decision. Many conflicts followed.

◀ Map of North America from 1826

The First Treaty

Settlers from Great Britain started signing **treaties** with the American Indians in the 1600s. The colonists wanted to own the land in the New World. To do this, they made agreements with the tribes.

American Indians did not see land in the same way as the settlers. The Indians thought the community should share the land. No one owned it. To the Indians, signing a treaty meant the settlers could use the land. The Indians did not believe they were giving the land to the settlers.

▼ **This document promised land in the New World to William Penn.**

William Penn was a British man who wanted to move to America. Before Penn left England, King Charles II gave him land in the colonies. When he got there, he saw that the Delaware Indians lived in his new home. He wanted to keep peace in the area. So, Penn asked to buy the land from the Indians.

The two sides agreed upon a price. This was the first treaty in America. The Delaware Indians respected Penn. Unlike others, he never broke the treaties he had with them.

William Penn

Talking with the Tribe

William Penn learned to speak the language of the Delaware Indians. He wanted to talk with the Indians without an **interpreter** (in-TER-pruh-tuhr). An interpreter was a person who translated between different languages.

Mr. Penn's Sons

William Penn had two sons who were not as honest as he was. The sons tricked the Delaware Indians. The sons said the Indians had signed another treaty with William Penn. The treaty supposedly said that Penn would get as much land as could be walked in a day and a half. Three men were chosen to walk as far as they could for a day and a half. One man walked 65 miles (105 km). The Delaware Indians felt cheated.

▲ These men earned land for William Penn's sons.

Early Treaties

Treaties with American Indians became common over the years. Some were made peacefully. The government would offer to buy land from the Indians. New land would be given in exchange.

The Indian tribes often ran into problems with these treaties. Sometimes more than one tribe would claim they owned an area. Other times, the chief would sign a treaty without the tribe's permission. Chiefs were often given gifts if they signed the treaties.

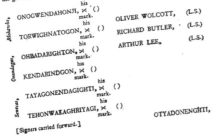

Example of a treaty from 1785

▲ **Signatures on a treaty**

Treaties Changed

In early treaties, Indians were in charge of their own land. If a person crossed into their area, the tribe could "punish him as they pleased." In later treaties, the United States handled problems differently. The Indians had to give lawbreakers to the United States government. It did not matter what race the lawbreakers were. They would be judged by United States laws.

Chiefs such as this ▶ one were very important to the success of a tribe.

In 1814, the United States government began a new **campaign** (cam-PAIN). It had plans to move five of the largest tribes out West. Treaty after treaty was signed, but the tribes did not want to move. They signed the documents just to make the government happy. Since no one was making the Indians leave, most of them stayed in the East.

Many Indians began acting like white settlers. They hoped that if they farmed or owned slaves, they could stay on their land.

The Indian Removal Act

In 1830, Congress passed the Indian Removal Act. This law gave the president the right to force the tribes to move west. It affected all tribes living east of the Mississippi River. Any tribe could be moved to Indian Territory.

Indian Territory was land on the west side of the Mississippi River. It was land that was **reserved** for the tribes. This is why the word *reservation* is used to describe where the tribes lived. The government promised that white settlers would never be allowed there.

The Five Civilized Tribes

The Cherokee, Chickasaw, Choctaw, Creek, and Seminole were called the "Five Civilized Tribes" by the white settlers. These tribes were "civilized" because they began to give up their Indian culture. They started acting like white settlers.

Indian Removal Act ▶
from 1830

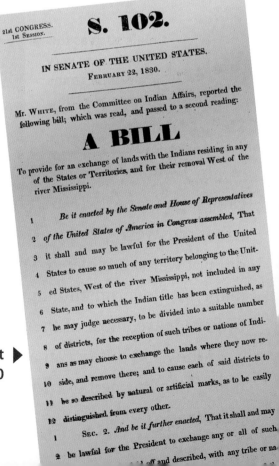

21st CONGRESS.
1st SESSION.

S. 102.

IN SENATE OF THE UNITED STATES.
FEBRUARY 22, 1830.

Mr. WHITE, from the Committee on Indian Affairs, reported the following bill; which was read, and passed to a second reading:

A BILL

To provide for an exchange of lands with the Indians residing in any of the States or Territories, and for their removal West of the river Mississippi.

1 Be it enacted by the Senate and House of Representatives
2 of the United States of America in Congress assembled, That
3 it shall and may be lawful for the President of the United
4 States to cause so much of any territory belonging to the Unit-
5 ed States, West of the river Mississippi, not included in any
6 State, and to which the Indian title has been extinguished, as
7 he may judge necessary, to be divided into a suitable number
8 of districts, for the reception of such tribes or nations of Indi-
9 ans as may choose to exchange the lands where they now re-
10 side, and remove there; and to cause each of said districts to
11 be so described by natural or artificial marks, as to be easily
12 distinguished from every other.
1   SEC. 2. And be it further enacted, That it shall and may
2 be lawful for the President to exchange any or all of such

Runaway Hideout

The land called the Indian Territory was also home to some runaway slaves from the East. The runaway slaves felt that it was a safe place to hide from their owners.

Slaves who escaped from ▶ southern plantations traveled west to be safe.

Individual Indians did not have to move with their tribes. The government agreed to give Indians United States **citizenship** (SIT-uh-zuhn-ship) if they stayed in the East and were productive. Some members of the tribes tried that way of life. Most of these tribe members soon missed their native **culture** (KUHL-chuhr). So, they joined their tribes out West.

At that time, no one believed the United States would get bigger. No one thought settlers would ever want to live west of the Mississippi River. They were wrong.

Moving West

Bands of Choctaw (CHOK-taw) Indians signed a treaty with the United States government. Not all members of the tribe moved, though. Some Choctaw decided to stay in Mississippi and try to fit in. Living like white settlers was difficult for the Indians. Over time, nearly all the Choctaw tribe members moved to reservations.

Not long after, the Chickasaw (CHIK-uh-saw) Indians signed a treaty and moved, too. They lived with the Choctaw. The Chickasaw paid the Choctaw to stay on their land.

The Seminole (SEM-uh-nuhl) and the Creek were not going to go as easily. They did not give up their homeland without a fight. After many bloody battles, both tribes were eventually moved to Indian Territory.

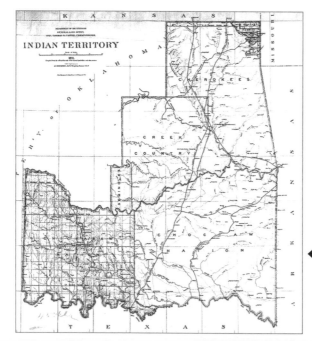

Bitter Journey

One group of Choctaw Indians moved west in 1831. During their trip, they were caught in a terrible winter storm. Many members of the tribe had to walk barefoot in the snow for 24 hours.

◀ This map shows how the tribes were settled on reservations in Indian Territory.

Death on the Trail

The Trail of Tears was called "The Place Where They Cried" by the Cherokee. It was a terribly rough journey. Many people died from sickness and poor conditions.

▼ Cherokee Indians on the Trail of Tears

Some Cherokee (CHAIR-uh-key) Indians signed a treaty to move without the agreement of the rest of the tribe. The government **ratified** it anyway. They were given two years to move the entire tribe. Since many of them had not agreed with the treaty, they refused to leave. Government troops came to remove them. The Cherokee people did not even have time to gather their belongings. They had to walk miles and miles. The long walk became known as the Trail of Tears.

Red Cloud's War

The Lakota (luh-CO-tuh) Indians lived in the area that is now North Dakota, South Dakota, Montana, and Wyoming. This area had plenty of bison for both the Indians and settlers. The white settlers did not bother the Indians very often. That changed when gold was discovered in the region.

Two mountain men mapped out a route called the Bozeman Trail. This trail went right through the Lakota territory. To get to the gold, miners began traveling the route in large numbers.

A Lakota chief, Red Cloud, wanted the Bozeman Trail closed. Miners and wagons disturbed the bison. Hunting became more difficult. The Lakota began to threaten everyone using the trail. The travelers asked for government protection.

▼ Chief Red Cloud

What's in a Name?

In most history books, Sioux is the name used to describe many of the tribes who lived in the northern plains states. However, the Indians themselves prefer to be called by their own tribal names—Dakota, Nakota, and Lakota. They do not want to go by a name given to them by someone else.

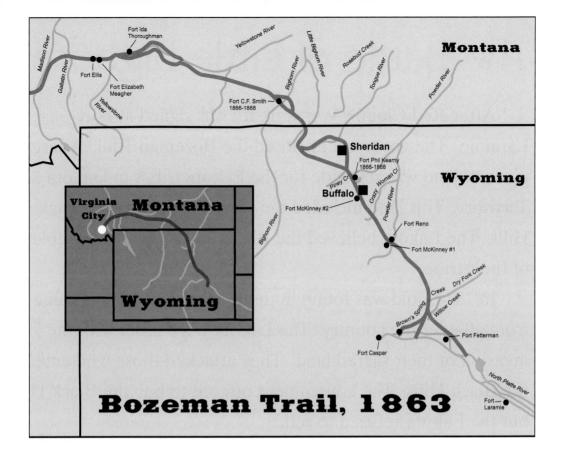

Bozeman Trail, 1863

United States government **officials** (uh-FISH-uhlz) knew they had to do something. They did not want the miners to be attacked along the trail. The government met with Red Cloud and other chiefs to find a solution. During the meeting, Red Cloud noticed army troops on the trail. The troops were building forts. Red Cloud realized that the meeting did not really matter. The government planned to keep the trail open. He was furious!

The Lakota bands joined together and attacked the forts. Many soldiers were killed. The government found it too hard to protect the trail. The army left and the Lakota burned down the forts. This was an important victory for Red Cloud and his people.

The Battle of Little Bighorn

After Red Cloud's War, a treaty was signed at Fort Laramie. The government closed the Bozeman Trail. A large piece of land was set aside for the Lakota tribes in Dakota Territory. This land included the **sacred** (SAY-kruhd) Black Hills. The Lakota believed the Black Hills were the birthplace of their tribe.

In 1874, gold was found in the Black Hills. Miners came from all over the country. The Lakota were upset with the invasion of their sacred land. They attacked those who entered the Black Hills. The government offered to buy the Black Hills, but the Lakota refused to sell.

Payment for the Black Hills

In 1923, the Lakota sued the United States for taking the Black Hills. Fifty-six years later, the courts decided the Lakota should get payment. The tribe was awarded $105 million. The Lakota refused to take the money. They did not want to be paid, they wanted the land back.

▲ The Black Hills in Dakota Territory

Remembering the Battle

In 1991, a memorial was created for the Indians who lost their lives at Little Bighorn. The name of the battlefield was also changed from Custer Battlefield National Monument to Little Bighorn National Monument.

George A. Custer

▼ Battle of Little Bighorn

Lakota Chief Sitting Bull moved his band to their summer camp along the Little Bighorn River. There were Cheyenne (shy-AN) Indians in camp as well. The United States Army sent troops to force them back to the reservation.

General George Custer was famous from his years fighting in the Civil War. He marched his troops hard and led his men in an attack against the Lakota Indians. There were many more Indians than Custer expected. General Custer and his men lost the battle and their lives.

Chief Joseph and the Nez Percé

The chief of the Nez Percé (NEZ PUHRS) Indians signed a treaty in 1855. It gave his people a reservation in Oregon and Idaho. Later, gold was found on the Nez Percé land. So, the government wanted to change the **boundaries** (BOUN-duh-rees). They wanted to make the reservation smaller.

A new treaty was written, but the chief would not sign it. He did not want to give up any of his tribe's land. When he died in 1871, his son became the new chief. This new chief's name was Chief Joseph.

The Red Napoleon

American newspapers called Chief Joseph "The Red Napoleon." They thought he was great at leading battles. Today, some historians believe that other Nez Percé Indians were actually in charge of the battles. Chief Joseph was mainly in charge of speaking for the tribe.

Chief Joseph of the Nez Percé ▶

Chief Joseph tried to get the government to change its mind. However, the white settlers were not giving up. They kept pushing for land. Eventually, some young Nez Percé **warriors** (WOR-yuhrs) got frustrated and attacked white settlers. Immediately, the United States military came to force the Nez Percé to move.

The Nez Percé tried to escape to Canada. They were on the move for over three months and 1,400 miles (2,250 km). Chief Joseph led his band in many small battles against the army. The Nez Percé finally **surrendered** (suh-REN-duhrd) only 40 miles (64.4 km) from the Canadian border.

When he surrendered, Chief Joseph made a speech that has become famous. At the end of his speech, he said, "Hear me, my chiefs! I am tired. My heart is sick and sad. From where the sun now stands, I will fight no more forever."

▼ The Nez Percé surrendering to the army

Ghost Dance

Like many tribes, Lakota Indians were not happy on the reservations. They wanted their old way of life again. A **ceremony** (SER-uh-mo-nee) called the Ghost Dance became popular. They danced because it made them feel closer to the way things used to be. It united them and showed that they were still one tribe.

The government was nervous about the Ghost Dance. They thought this dance was a form of rebellion. Troops were sent to calm the Indians. The military leaders also wanted to question Lakota Chief Sitting Bull. They knew he was a great leader in the Lakota tribe. Maybe he could help stop this ceremony.

Dancing the Ghost Dance

The Ghost Dance was different from the usual Indian dances. There were no drums. The steps started slow, like shuffling, then got faster and faster. Most unusual was that women and children were allowed to join in

Sitting Bull knew about the Ghost Dance because it was part of his tribe's culture. But, he was not encouraging the tribe to do the dance. Lakota police arrested him. Sitting Bull's friends tried to free him. A Lakota policeman was shot. As he fell to the ground, he fired his gun. The bullet hit Sitting Bull in the chest. Another policeman, Red Tomahawk, shot Sitting Bull in the back of the head. The great Lakota chief was dead.

◀ Chief Sitting Bull of the Lakota Indians

Sitting Bull's Vision

Sitting Bull had mystical **visions** in his life. In one, a meadowlark told him that his own people would kill him. This bothered him greatly. Over the years, he told this story many times. It's sad that his vision came true when the Lakota police officers killed him.

The Massacre at Wounded Knee

Another Lakota chief, Big Foot, heard about Sitting Bull's death. Although Big Foot was an old man, the government wanted to capture him. He decided to find Chief Red Cloud on the Pine Ridge Reservation in the Dakota Territory. Chief Red Cloud had promised other Indians protection from the army.

As Chief Big Foot and his band were making their way to the Pine Ridge Reservation, army troops stopped them. The band surrendered. They were taken to Wounded Knee Creek for the night.

▼ Diagram of the Battle of Wounded Knee

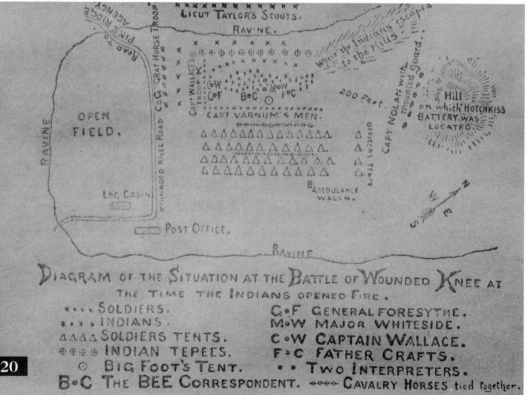

The next day, soldiers demanded that the tribe give up all its weapons. The Lakota Indians were searched and treated roughly. One Lakota man refused to give up his weapon. A soldier tried to take his gun, and it fired into the air. A battle began. Many Indians were not able to defend themselves because they had no weapons. Hundreds of men, women, and children were killed.

Wounded Knee Protest

Eighty-three years after Wounded Knee, the Lakota Indians organized a protest. They wanted the government to look at all Indian treaties. They felt that the Indians had been cheated out of much of their land.

▼ The Wounded Knee Massacre

A Young Chief Big Foot

Life on the Reservation

American Indians fought against going to the reservations. This way of living was very different from the freedom they had enjoyed. They wanted the right to roam in the same regions they always had.

At first, reservations were simply pieces of land saved for the tribes. The Indians could do as they pleased, but only in their assigned areas. Later, reservations were set up as small communities. **Agents** were hired to be in charge. Their job was to pass out food and supplies sent by the government. The agents were also supposed to protect the tribe and teach them skills. Sadly, many of the agents were not honest men. They hurt the tribes instead of helping the Indians.

◀ Places were set up on the reservations for distributing food and other items.

Boarding School

Some American Indian children were taught at boarding schools. The goals of these schools were to teach the Indian children the ways of white settlers. The students learned to speak English as well as read and write.

The Biggest Reservation

There are about 275 Indian reservations in the United States today. The largest is the Navajo reservation. It is in part of three different states—Arizona, New Mexico, and Utah.

▲ Pine Ridge Reservation in South Dakota

Today Indian reservations still exist. Tribal members now run the reservations. The reservations are like small nations. Most even have constitutions to define their rules and way of life.

The 1800s were a painful time for the American Indians. It is hard to imagine how it felt to be forced onto reservations. The tribes held very strong beliefs about their ways of life. They believed that no one owned the land. Indians wanted to share and respect the land's resources. American Indian cultures have changed over the years, but many tribes continue proudly today.

Glossary

agents—people sent by the government to work on the reservations

bands—smaller parts of a tribe who live and work together

boundaries—outer limits of an area of land

campaign—plan of events in order to reach a goal

ceremony—an event performed because of a tradition or custom

citizenship—having membership to a state or country

culture—way of behaving that is the same for a whole group of people

interpreter—person who translates between different languages

officials—people in charge

ratified—officially agreed upon or approved

reservations—lands set aside especially for Indians to live and work

reserved—set aside or saved

sacred—holy or worthy of respect

surrendered—gave up power or control

treaties—agreements or contracts between groups

visions—dreams that tell of the future; these can happen when you are asleep or awake

warriors—young, brave Indian men who fought to protect their tribes